MW01658039

THE DREAM GIVERS

by Margo LaGattuta

cover artist, Chris Reising
cover artist, Peter Knox
lay-out editor, Wayne Spelius
editor-at-large, Carol Spelius

LAKE SHORE PUBLISHING

373 Ramsay Road

Deerfield, IL 60015

Copyright, 1990
ISBN #0-941363-12-0
Library of Congress
#PS3562. A3126D 74 1990
811' . 54 -- dc20
$8.95

". . . archetype
of the world always a step
beyond the world, that can't
be looked for, only
as the eye wanders,
found. . ."

Denise Levertov

This book is dedicated to my parents,
Ed and Betty Grahn,
who taught me how to dream.

FOREWORD

This book was given to me by my dreams. It had its beginning in the unfiltered images and sounds that bubble up from sleep or the flash of a daydream. The poems allow themselves to develop as a kind of dialogue between the concious and the unconcious. a process sometimes called active imagination or lucid dreaming. I have used this method in teaching writing workshops, where we form a dream circle to call up the engaging metaphors or myths in our dreams, share our associations, then use them to trigger writing.

But the poems sleep until they are read or heard. They come wrapped in the breath of our connected images. So I invite you on this journey with me.

Margo LaGattuta

Table of Contents

I SWEET LIMITATIONS

II RIDING TOUGH HORSES

III EVERYTHING REAL KEEPS MOVING

I SWEET LIMITATIONS

JUNK MAIL

Dear MARGO LA GATTUTA:
a free FM stereo earphone radio
and a, one time only, free
spinal examination by Dr. Mark
Endall, can be yours
just for the asking. This
limited time offer, for
MARGO LA GATTUTA only,
can be had post haste.

Send us this detached card
that has your special number
on it: 11566493.
Say, "Yes, I MARGO LA GATTUTA
would like to examine the
SOLAR SYSTEM as my
introduction to PLANET EARTH.
I want my ten days free examination.
I want some future volumes,
under the terms in the
accompanying letter.

IMPORTANT --
I MARGO LA GATTUTA
will remain free
to cancel my subscription to
PLANET EARTH at any time.
I will send no money now.
This offer expires.

SWEET LIMITATIONS

The Mayor of Benzonia
is looking for a bride.
Far and wide he gathers servants
to scour the earth for her.

"She must have little feet,"
he measures, "so she needn't
tip toe in the begonia garden,
but not too tiny to stroll
wide-eyed through the impatiens."

"Look for long shiny hair,"
he dreams, "to reflect the fern,
the climbing gloxinia, but no
tangles I could get lost in."

The Mayor of Benzonia begins
his list of preferred body parts.
Like a dress maker he measures
where to let her out,
how much to take her in.

He draws a model bride
on graph paper, labeling the eyes
two blue lakes: Lake Erie
and the Ole Woman Cove of the Chesapeake Bay.

He names the teeth *like pearlshells*,
the immortal flow of breath,
a wind blowing through them
from the nurturing southwest.

He draws her making sago flour,
a prerequisite to the kneading.
She must bring him two loaves
for his breakfast of coffee and oranges.

The mayor of Benzonia sighs
at the joy of wanting her.
"I will spare nothing," he thinks.
"I will pay any price."

He waits for the maidens
who parade before him daily
dressed in white gauze pinafores,
their feet shod in crystal pumps.

He waits for the one, the only one,
who can bring him grapes and
yogurt for his indigestion. He waits,
now anxious, now halting,

for the bride with wire-rimmed glasses,
the near-sighted one who
sees into everything,
but not too far.

WINTER SILKS

Shopping by mail has never
been easier. There are sales
and I, who always like a bargain,
want to buy something soft for less,

some luxurious white silk camisole,
a deluxe weight striped cowl turtle neck
or, just right for office or evening,
I'll take a pair of raw silk slacks

made from rare spun cocoons
gathered from the Asian wilds, then
processed by hand. "A pleasure to touch,"
the catalogue says, "as shown with only

a slight defect or two. The fabric is more
heavily speckled than our specifications."
I probably want this more than a kiss.
"Comfortable because it breathes" I read,
"and is surprisingly easy to care for."

I'm shaking now, with desire for the
hand washable Crepe de Chine shirt
(use a cool iron to smooth out wrinkles).
I want it more than I want
your hand on my shoulder.

I've grasped my VisaCard, positioned
my finger on the Touchtone dial.
"Wait just a minute," I snap,
"Where are your scruples? What room
have you got in your drawers for all this?"

I try to calm myself.
"Remember starving children in Detroit.
Remember your flickering bank balance,
your easy charge limit, your expiration date."

"It seems to be working," I muse.
I'm having a submerged epiphany
at the thought of not buying.
Nothing new to make me sad
when it arrives and the arms don't fit.

I'm proud of myself this time.
I don't call and I'm still not calling.
Not even a final clearance can get to me.
Not even a pair of featherlight silk
glove liners for commuting in frigid weather.

JESUS AT THE OUTLET

Shoes grow wild at the Village
Outlet discount store. Red pumps,
gray and black patent leather,
high heeled sling-backs,
wedgie blue and tassled
cowboy boots, a soft silver

slipper. All thc fancy
footwear you could ever dream
fills rooms and spreads
onto window sills and up
the stairs. Boxes and boxes
of sandals, like Jesus shoes,

wait to be tried on, as women
browse and ponder. They size
up the situation, reach size sevens
on tip toe from the top
of the dusty shelf.

A young girl begs
her mother for sequined
tennis shoes. "You'll have
to wait," she's told. "If Jesus
wants you to have "em,
they'll still be here."

White paint peels off the wall
above the plastic thongs.
The Village Outlet is made
from an old church building.
Through the layers and years
Jesus' face peeks through.

He is watching the pink
canvas tongues, the laces
getting done and undone.
He sees the ladies bag all
their dreams in paper.

The maintenance men try painting
over the face of Jesus,
but He just keeps coming back.
It gets a little brighter
each time around His eyes.
The last one to close the store
at night says a funny sound

like a sigh seems to rise
up somewhere behind the loafers.

POET IN THE DEPARTMENT STORE

They put me in leisure wear,
next to the appliqued jogging suits,
with a sign saying, "Meet
local poet," and a pile of my books.

Shoppers amble by, afraid
of my eyes. "Don't look
at a poet too close,"
they think. It's easier

to stare at last year's
swim suits - half off.
I'm selling wierdness, something
real all over my face.

Who wants to buy
a little mistake, the dream
that fell over, the fly
in yesterday's pudding?

Got a minute while I
sweat, or carry on
about the truth? Admit
a weakness you've repressed?

With any ten dollar purchase
you get this gift set free:
five stanzas on loneliness,
a pithy couplet on retreat.

Hey, here's my final offer:
a cut crystal dream vision,
archetypal journey toward
Nirvana or the Holy Mall.

Take me home. I'll give you
ten shudders and a look
at a long forgotten wish.
Let me be your picture window.

Or at least throw me
into a CARE package for your
rich aunt Sylvia. The one who
has everything, but it's not enough.

AN OPEN LETTER FROM A DISTANT PLACE

This is not your letter,
so why are you reading it?
I am not writing to you from Lansing this time,
because I know you aren't home.
I keep buying post cards.
I can't help it.
I erase them and steam off the stamps
so you can't find me.
This is so far away from Fargo.
There are barely trees here,
and sometimes a bird.
This is the last time
I'm going to tell you about the woodpecker.
The way my dog chewed up a small dachshund.
Forget it.
I can't believe you're still reading this.
Don't you know the cold weather is over?
It keeps raining here.
I forgot my glasses,
and I had to put my contact lenses
in two water glasses,
making sure I could find the right
one next morning.
I can see you don't mind my candor.
My plane from Knoxville was held over,
and my suitcase went to Memphis.

You would have been proud of me.
I didn't yell "shit-heads" like the man in front of me
in the lost baggage line.
There are no night gowns,
so I'm having to sleep naked.
I've asked the desk clerk for a wake-up call
just to hear my phone ring.
I can't tell you about the law suit
or how the oral surgeon is treating my dry socket.
The hole is so deep you won't believe it.

DEAF KITTEN

He looks this way and that
with no sound to follow,
only what his eye can catch.

He cocks his head,
one ear twitching.
He turns round and round, as if
waiting to hear some radio,

a distant long range
of music, wasted on
blank ears that won't
tune in.

No one can call
a deaf kitten, though they
stand behind him and shout
out of the wild periphery.

The white kitten
cries out, as he runs.
He sees only the day in front,
the bent sticks
among the leaves.

PUPPET FACE

Some think I'm free, but I'm
going nowhere without you.
Make my lips move
and tell me what to say.

This is the glitter, the show,
the empty dance with all the strings.
Put your hand inside
and watch me do my eyes.

I have no arms, no way
to move without your holding.
My broken face hides secrets
you must tell me not to tell.

HEART RUMOR

To cry out is to love
when it hurts a little.
The heart opens down
into interior rooms.

There is a table,a chair,
two lamps, and a window.
The lover walks in velvct slippers
along the papered walls.

He lies down in a pose
reminiscent of a mound of roses.
His bones forever rest
bodyless in the thumping room,

rumored to be gone and
attended still
only by a cast of visitors.

HOME MOVIE

A bath gets me going. "Nothing comes from an idle mind," my boss used to say. Or, "Idle time is wasted time. Do something now." In the tub, I show myself a movie of this. Me cleaning the kitchen. Me driving to the bank. going shopping, fixing the sink, rushing to work, making phone calls. It's a fast movie, without an ending. I show it again and again, looking for the plot. In one scene, I'm all alone in the bath tub, and there is no sound. My son knocks on the door. His lips form the words, "Are you in there? It's the water softener guy on the phone."

AND ALWAYS THERE ARE TRAINS

(for J.L.)

How good, how very good
we are inside trains.
We eat there. Have our
cold meals laid out, our napkins
folded like bed linens
around our foam rubber lives.

We are obedient in trains.
We sit in clean compartments.
Wait to have our ticket punched.
Wait for someone to reach out
for our stub, our pass,
our fingered time sheet.

Erect and hopeful, we sit in
lower berths near a window,
watch tree and pasture slip by,
blue hill blur into lake and weed,
streak of red sky flying.

We let trains carry us asleep
from one stop to the next.

TO NATALIE WOOD, LEAVING THE BOAT

Wait, Natalie. Come back.
We could be friends.
I always thought you were
so thin and had
those beautiful eyes.
I thought you were happy.
You have a rich husband,
and you love your kids.
You have your job.
My God, I couldn't
know you. But I was
wrong, Natalie. Don't jump.

I'm in the Palace
ordering the soup of the day.
A woman in a cloth coat
is crying, and a friend
is handing her a pill.
At another table, a woman
reads your headline and orders
chocolate cake. Natalie, don't jump.

I see you perched there
in that little boat.
I see you are real.
You watch your old films
on fast forward
as you lean into the water.

Natalie, we could have lunch.
You could call me.

WET LEAVES

The maple trees bend low
with leaves like wet laundry
drooping down the window pane.
Water is hanging heavy on their backs.

Even a slight breeze
has a hard time ruffling
this gravitational pull.
Waterlogged sweaters they wear,
the air holes knitted with rain.

"Even sweaters should be blocked,"
I say. "Think of the arm holes,
the necks all out of shape.
Autumn is closing in and
leaves will be almost falling."

Nothing that comes from the sky
can be blocked. It's like trying
to hold back a sneeze. The rain
comes down around us fully.
We cup our hands and watch.

THE BLIND WOMAN'S HOUSE

Forgetting, she puts down her purse
on the ironing board. In five steps
will be the sink, the habits she must
go through to find the fern, the
water, the cup, the paper towel.

Climbing the stair lightly, she must
count her way to the top, measuring air
with each foot lifted. Things must be
taken in sets of three: three turns

to the bathroom. Three closed windows
to the one that cranks open. Three
steps from the glazed sofa to the
lamp. Without eyes she counts
three snaps of light into her evening.

No one knows her blindness better
than she does. She sees it as a kind
of comfortable home, a way
to believe in the placing of things,
a way of counting on borders.

The map of her life is perfect.
Nothing more than she touches
could ever be there. No lover
with eyes could see her
darkness. No habit of hands
could touch her light.

STRIPPED DOWN

She works the bars in Windsor, she
is lithe and borderless, her skin
tighter than paper money. She
likes to be called Mouse, her

gray feet soft on the runway
carpet. Silent movement in
dark rooms always got her
noticed. But now the dance is

too fast, she doesn't even start
with rings or feathers anymore,
but opens bare and walks
in real cold. Won't attach herself

to anyone's eyes, but gazes
at the torn velvet wallpaper,
thinks it curls like
fingers around a glass of beer.

She paws the air filled with a
memory of lost cities, and a
nameless hotel lobby. How she
once played it out in

hesitation. How she
loved to slither in silk scarves
for what they came to see.
Only one color of loss at a time.

How she didn't used to give them
breath til the last minute.
When the dream dropped down on her ankles,
when light flashed on her hair and was gone.

I BRAKE FOR SUNSETS

(for Erik)

The night we sat in the sunset
bats were flying all around.
Venus was the only light
shining in the fallen sky.

You, playing the recorder,
reminded me of lost bats,
the bats of your childhood
drawn in Magic Marker on your hands,

the Batman cape I made you,
the rubber bats I bought
in the magic store in Berkley,
all the bats you needed to escape.

I wanted to save you from bats,
keep bats out of your hair,
help you get over bat invasions,
make you a bat cake for your birthday.

Bats were a joke between us once,
but you were more serious than I.
You bet me bats were coming for us.
You saw them first and ducked.

THE BEDROOM

Nothing is ever found in that wretched room.
Even the crying, the fierce
pounding on pillows, the calls,
the lost moaning soaked into the walls
have been sponged forever from our ears.
And what a pileup of junk!
Lingerie, once alive and breathing,
old hats, purses, layers of long
overdue books block the traffic.
Each lost thing has begun to grow on us.
Even a small slip has its mourning.

LUCKY MARKET

Because you left me,
and I am all out of cranberry tea,
I race to find the Lucky Market.

In the Nugget Diner parking lot,
I ask a man who is pushing
a Universal wheel chair for directions.

The man points west. The woman
in the chair points east.

He is drunk and she is pissed.
Everything spins inside this moment.
It is late, almost too late
now for buying tea.

Some days I just can't get enough,
and everything I need closes.
Around any corner might be
nothing I know.

DREAMER'S FURNITURE

Sometimes, staring out a winter window, I forget even the names of things. *Curtain, tree, prairie* . . . all drift through my senses like so much snow falling through wordy air.

"How do I call this?" I wonder, as I try to build rooms around each floating thought. And if the naming comes easy, I trick myself. I rearrange all the furniture so that each room looks like nowhere I've been. So that anyone passing through might recognize a familiar couch. Might sit for awhile in my dream, forgetting the names of things in alphabetical order. The couch inside the couch becomes anyone's picture window. Becomes anyone's own snow.

II RIDING TOUGH HORSES

RIDING TOUGH HORSES

From the bottom
of my dream of horses
I come shining.

They fly high and wide
in my night window,
galloping muscle and flank.
White and brown,
sweaty pink nostriled.

The sound first,
a loud beating in dirt.
Then the bodies,
elastic and turning
sharp right hand turns,
bending back on themselves.

I see the spray of hair,
mane and tail spread
in slow motion.

This dream is firm
and never gets easy.
I hold to the curves,
crack the tipping snow fence.

I get alive this way.
I rise up to it.

IMAGE POWDER

Grasping something cellular
I gather particles. Only
this fine dust becomes
a tree, a gravel path
just outside a dream
landscape, the interior
always calling out for
more color, some
fine seeing on my
part, only slow to soak
in, a kind of music
that invents itself,
the shadow dancing with
its own blue silk scarf,
a breeze alive in gauze
fabric making waves,
allowing me
allowing me in.

DREAMSCAPE I

Hot night in Lake Orion.
We lie like two loaves
of unbaked bread
rising in the dark.

There is much to beware of:
my arm, your thought,
a leg over my belly.
What I am is silver,

and I spoon into
your closed eye.
You crack your knuckles
and stretch. There are
crickets singing of
long-legged silences.

Darkness, a June bug,
crawls around our bed.
Your breathing stitches the air.
Stiff arms get folded like envelopes.
Your dream, like paper,
slips into mine.

DREAMSCAPE II

I dream of scissors
cutting open the landscape,
play paper dolls with the sun,
and slip it into a red horizon line.

I make little outfits for the trees.
What they wear to church.
What they dance in.
Every day I make a new picture.

Sometimes I get dizzy
and have to trim the hedges.
This dream gives me one star
at a time to paste
over a languid sky.

I enter the scene like water,
try to flood
the edges of the frame.

PERIOD HOMES

Some dreams are houses.
Houses with dark mediterranean
furniture in dank airless rooms.
Houses with artful strangers lurking
in period costume among the cobwebbed
lace doilies. Empty houses. Houses
with no lamps lit. Robbed houses
with unretrieved losses: a crusty
loaf of rye bread. Houses on stilts
with no foundation. Houses with
eyes that look over a dim lake
where the black dragon swims, and
none of us dares to get wet.

Some dreams take place in the sky:
airplane with trailing rope ladder
and me, an aerial ballerina,
swinging through a cloud,
the crowd below me politely aghast.

Flying is simple. I click
my heels and something in me rises.
Something glistens and I know all sounds
become windows. Something in me
alive and full of night
sings.

FALLEN MOUTH OVER LONG WINDOWS

The night the mouth fell we were sitting expectantly. We were waiting to hear it land. We were quiet as mice. It began to spill words: *and, if, maybe, window, door, silk robe*. Just the hiss of the sounds made us shudder. The mouth was embarrassed. It wanted to stop, regroup, gather itself. But, no, it was on a roll: *fox, overview, wallet, androgony, artichoke, fudge.* It got frisky, made itself circular and began to whistle.

Some of us felt comforted by the loosening of our ears. Some got up and went to our rooms to forget. We kept waiting for the mouth to tire, fill itself so full of its own juices that it might be catapulted right into silence.

But no, it forged forward: *flow, Afghanistan, manger, diaphanous, albeit, reindeer*. We looked out over the long windows to another mouth, that was curled up to a whisper. *Sh-h-h-h*, it seemed to signal. We saw a meadow in the distance. Something waved like flags of surrender. We kept listening for the last vibrational hum before the scent of plum roses allowed us to enter the unexpected light.

SILENT WOMEN UNDER THE SAND

They've been there for centuries, their mouths full of gritty thoughts, lips stuck in long silent sentences that go all the way back to the sea. It started with children playing. They built a whole town in the sand. Then waves came in to bury everyone. Women were standing in rows in white Confirmation dresses when the water hit. They were trying to sing, but words were dry and lost before reaching the air. They formed a mum chorus, harmonizing thoughts without notes. They turned themselves into stiff castles. Now and again, as waves rolled over their heads, small starched bonnets would be uncovered on the beach. Anyone walking by might pick one up, lift it to his ear like a shell or a curtain. Perhaps listen to a distant quiet window.

PAINTING FACES

Make me a rainbow, they say.
Each one lifts his face high
trusts it in the palm of my hand.
And I want stars around my eyes.

There is no stillness like a child
who holds her face so still
she feels the dance of clowns
circling her nose in red paint.

I have all the power of blue
in my right hand. I can
color in tears, make a face
of sad flowers on a stem.

I can make it rain
until the sun comes out
on this cheek or that.
Draw a garden of lips.

Color me a camouflage face,
one green-eyed boy asks.
And I make him disappear
in a jungle of olive and brown.

He looks in a mirror
to face the inside forest.
Safe in the color of old leaves
he goes hiding.

Painting faces is an odd
old task. They come
to me and I make them
go away fast.

Children want me to do it.
Erase me, they say.
Color me in wild.
I want to scare you.

THINKING LIKE A TREE

I am the willow tree in the garden of your childhood. I stand over you with my arms out, crying. I am all that is left of your first life. I watched your mother bat a birdie back and forth, back and forth across a net. I remember your first boyfriend, Bill. He let her win, hoping to charm her, so he could win you.

Cars go by. The dust of Darramoor Road settles on my long leaves. I wait each day for more rain, so I won't die of this thirst. I keep wondering where you are, how far you've drifted from the doll house your father built under me. I see your cats return again and again. They whine at the empty house. I can feel the longing as they run up my trunk.

Someday you will stop, anywhere on a dirt road, and know how strong I am, how full of yourself. How the soft green I still hold in my hands is your own spring.

I CAME BY A RIVER

and the journey flashed
through me like a light
year. Some electric sound
got me moving from
the original place over
mountains and dusty
windows outside of time.

I became a small shadow,
something anyone might have
missed. I began spinning
deep in tomorrow's orchard.

I came by a river
and the water keeps rising.
I came to begin something wild.

GOING ALL THE WAY

The aroma of old
lipstick sends me flying
back to Ocean City, Maryland,
to soft shelled crabs and butter
where I learned to walk the walk.

There Bonnie and I painted our faces,
tanned our fresh bodies.
Boys were out there
and we had red lips.

That was the Year of the Flood!
The Mastery of Kotex Belts!
rude awakening to blood stains,
a Girl Scout movie on cramps.

I landed under the boardwalk
with a sailor named Frank.
I dug my nails, "Fire and Ice"
by Revlon, into his back.

"Is this doing it?" I thought.
Mother said I could have babies
if I let any boys too close.
So I kept my clothes on,

squirmed out from under him.
If touching boys could do it
I might get pregnant on the bus.
Even in study hall I was afraid.

I stared at Brenda Starr necking
with her mystery man in bold print.
I hid their picture under my pillow.
"Look at 'em going all the way," I thought.

TELLING STORIES

I am wolf woman.
Out of my green eyes
flow the Arctic winds
that spin and whistle a tale for you.

First the halted howling,
then a tree dance enters,
and the story the tree tells
begins to tell me its versions.

And the mountains come running.
And all the wolves half way
up the mountains come running,
and the few who are half down.

And there is a moon story now.
The moon is telling it slow
like a raw onion peeling back
layers of story and story.

And watch my wolf ways.
Watch me exaggerate and hear
the tempo rush through us,
a black bird flutter in the heart.

Hear the bird story itself to us,
make a home in the bone
where every story wants to be held,
where every old story is breathing.

The black bird wants to fly
right in the eye of the wolf story.
And the long sky opens
to swallow the tale whole.

ANOTHER POEM ABOUT THE SEA

In a blue mood again, the mad sea begins pulling at his curled white hair. He is just about worn out from crying for lost time. Wailing into a white lace hanky, the sea wonders if it's too late to change his life. He is so tired. The old fishermen won't stop dragging nets over his shallow places, sailing boats through his face. He wishes there were more stars in his future. He gets bored. And the moon always pulling at him.

III EVERYTHING REAL KEEPS MOVING

"*Except for the point. the still point,*
There would be no dance, and there is only the dance."

. . . T.S.Eliot

LOOKING FOR ELVIS IN KALAMAZOO

He's been spotted in the Maypole
Diner, sipping coffee with the regulars.
He wears white sox and penny loafers,
stone washed jeans and a button down.

Elvis has gone real on us.
He might be anyone now.
He's discovered oat bran and thrown away
his sequins for a cotton blend.

Elvis is hiding in the Burger King
playing chess with someone's grampa.
He doesn't even win sometimes.
He wants to be plainer than a fish sandwich.

Hordes of women in their forties
prowl the streets with their eyes peeled.
They've traced him with divining rods
to the front lobby of the Harris Hotel.

Hiking up their Underalls,
they dream of one last look at a star.
They watch the lips of the aging bell boys
for that famous quiver, that stray curl.

They know Elvis can't hide forever
under plain wraps in Kalamazoo.
Any moment now he'll slip out
and shiver in his ordinary pants.

THE WISH BRACELET

"The way to love anything is to realize
that it might be lost.". . . Fortune Cookie

They say you tie it on your wrist
and wear it every minute,
even in the shower, or in a hurricane,
or in bed with your lover.

Mine is purple, green and orange
and came from Guatamala.
Mine is the color of joy,
the power of wishes tied in knots.

They say your dreams come true
the day the bracelet falls off.
My arm is heavy with the burden.
I carry the gift of loss around me.

I carry the gift of waiting
for small threads to fray,
for each color to begin bleeding,
for the friction dance on my skin.

To know wild colors now
is all hope in a circle.
Anything beautiful might be lost; I see
everything real keeps moving.

HOMECOMING

"FREED MAN FINDS RELEASE BITTERSWEET"
(Headline in Detroit Free Press, Nov.4,1986)

In the planned strategy
of isolation, a hostage
gets time to think over
all his crimes.

His captors invent
errors for him,
and, oh, he dreams of running
free on a California hillside.

The release is sudden,
an unexpected rush
of clean air, like the scent
of hyacinths in bloom.

Heading for home, family,
he smiles occasionally,
says he feels well,
but gives no detail.

He pictures that room,
daily green soup and bread,
the dish of hope he carried.
He wonders now

in the snarl of traffic,
the crush of welcome eyes,

if he'll ever be alone enough
to hear his heart open.

THE DREAM GIVERS

The dream givers live up there in the woodwork.
They are little people with eyes
that can see through walls.
As a child, I knew them by the shadows they left
as they scurried under my bed
or in my closet when I entered the room.

My sister, Susan, knew I had too many
on my side of the room we shared, so she snuck
around and piled some of mine up under her pillow.
"Don't worry," she said. "When I grow up I won't
do this."

The dream givers knew what I was looking for.
They waited in the attic insulation to entice me.
They wanted me to fall through the ceiling,
like mother warned me about. I knew I had to
fall through some day, into that other place.

Sometimes they still pull on my toes if I'm sleeping,
and the man I'm sleeping with scratches his nose.
They run all over his body, trying
to wiggle their way in.
If he is dreaming about the sea,
they bring their life jackets

and bob around on the waves of his slow breathing.
Nothing happens that they can't enter.
Even when I'm cutting cantaloupe, they sit perched
on the knife, and the fruit ripens with their singing.

Once Garin called them my prisoners,
said I should take them everywhere
and force them to listen to my stories.
He asked where he could go
to get his own set of prisoners.

But the dream givers can't be contained that way.
They fly around and snarl if I try to trap them.
Every new dream comes wrapped in their breath,
and none of the old dreams die without their mourning.

SEEING THINGS

Just now there is a gold star in my window. No one sees it but the man who comes to clean my furnace. "This won't take long," he says. "I need to blow out all your vents." As he reaches the one on the kitchen floor, the star catches his wandering eye.

"I used to drive a train," he says now. "Always on the same track for thirty years. Back and forth from New Haven to Manhattan. One day I looked up and saw the North Star. Then I knew it was time to pick apples."

We look together in the small bedroom
for a heater vent, and can't find one there.

Once in a while this happens. Something you've seen before turns up missing. A star that you have always seen is visible to someone else.

I get my furnace cleaned every year. And now this.

PLAYING BAGELS

When I eat bagels, I like to make pictures with the crumbs. The yellow flakes from an egg twist, a few black poppy seeds, a flake or two of caraway. If I move them around on the table, they might become a window into some future room. It must be how my grandmother felt looking into tea cups. First you see a journey, like a road twisting between two hills. Sometimes a traveler, but you can't make out the face. Or pirates, a hidden treasure, the family jewels.

But the crumbs are a looser game, not nailed down, like the freeze-frame left in a cup of Ty Phoo tea. And there's a freedom in the rearrangement. Even the uncertainty of an unexpected typhoon.

SHE EXAMINES FAME

Fame is not a horse, *she said.*
It doesn't take me where I want to go.
Fame is not the rider, or the whip.
There is no urging it on, no demanding it.

Some women are famous for their eyes, *she said*,
or for something orderly in their kitchen cabinets.
Some women are famous for their stillness,
for being so uncertain they speak in shadows.

Fame is not an elephant, *she said.*
It does not walk around in circles,
carrying so much weight.
Fame is more like David Hibling, master illusionist,
who will, in the course of the evening,

make a three thousand pound elephant disappear.
Fame is not a pair of high-heeled shoes
to make me stand taller on my
perfectly shaped ankles and calves.

Some women are afraid of fame.
They walk on tip toe into higher places,
till someone sees them, and they forget their names.
Some women forget to be inside their lives,

till it is almost too late.
Fame is not an airplane, *she said.*
It doesn't lift me above
all the ordinary people in the field,

but fame is more like Amelia Earhart,
who flew all around the world,
then vanished near Howland Island.
No one ever found her body, or the plane.

Fame is what goes away when it is held too tight.
Fame is the wedding of body, mind, and spirit,
the quest for wholeness that pulls us all toward light.
Fame, *she said*, is what follows us,
if we keep giving it away.

I AM NOT A WOMEN'S LIBBER

"The answer is 'Yes'. The question is
'How do we get there?'" . . . Sue Schooner

I love sweet midwestern men
with glistening eyes reading
poems about their children
in bay windows, their wives walking
toward them with long bare legs.

I love imagining my next
lover, the one who understands my
need for clutter, the way I have
wings to fly above the concrete sidewalk,
my need for standing on the doorstep alone.
I love the way he watches me secretely
from the bed of tomorrow. Waits for me to climb in.

I love my last lover,
the one who calls me at midnight,
his voice ringing velvet bells in my ear.
"Do you remember Chicago?" he purrs.
"No man could love your back
the way I do. Don't ever let another man
see your delicate feet."

I love my last husband
the one who took everything
even the bubinga bird cage
when he couldn't fit me in it
anymore. I love his
smooth brown skin, his eyes
a frozen gentleness more polished

than the redwood dining room table he built.

I love the engagement he brings
to each act, even the act
of separation. He does it pure,
uncluttered, like a clean room.

I love the clean businessman
who eats alone in restaurants,
the man in the office supply store
who lets me xerox myself
over and over, and never gets tired,
who winks at me when I buy
Manila envelopes to mail myself in.

I love my son's college roommate
who sleeps on our livingroom couch,
watches my legs from the corner of his closed eyes
as I readjust my slip.

I love all the men in audiences listening
who won't look at my scorched metaphors.
I love all the men in other women's poems,
the angry ones, the shy ones, the delicate
delicate husbands standing alone in the rain.

I love all the men standing outside waiting
for the women in prison at Camp Gilman,
the men who write letters: "I love you, Peggy.
It'll be O.K. The children are at your mother's.
I went to see your lawyer last Tuesday.
Don't give up, Peggy. I'll still be here
when you get out."

LEARNING TO DANCE BY MAIL

I'll have to get married soon
because I'm such a clumsy single.
I've tried all the singles haunts
even the dance at the Holiday Inn.

I've danced with long-necked Byron
who kept doing the box step.
I asked how old he was,
and did he believe that dentists
really have more fun?

"Oh, you live in Rochester,"
he said. "I really love
the malls up there. Do you
like to play Putt Putt Golf?"

Something in me was sinking
like the blind date in high school,
that hideous hayride with the jock.
I've thought of taking an ad out

like in the Personal column
of the Rochester Eccentric:
"Lonely poet who likes to eat
strawberries needs a friend."

If I could just
throw my hair back
and be a party animal
like Pat's friend Claudia.

She says, "This is work, you know.
You have to keep moving.
Pick out one you like
and ask if he's a Pisces."

I'd rather be in a bubble bath
reading SEX AND THE BRAIN.
I'd rather be doing the dishes
or doing the cha cha
with my fun cat Jim.

I'd rather be having my teeth cleaned
or watching "Gilligan's Island"
than here facing the music
doing the box step with Byron
and having so much fun.

NOTHING LIES LIKE THE TRUTH

I could never marry you.
I'm having a frisky affair
with a wild man named Geraldo from Brazil
who loves eating kiwis off my eyelids.

I could never marry you.
I'll soon be off for Tibet
where I have a scholarship to Swami School
and eight gurus will be fighting over my aura.

I could never marry you.
I'm leading an experiential workshop
on letting go of all relationships
on a mountain top in Lima, Peru.

I could never marry you.
I'm getting a Ph.D. in androgony.
I've learned to meditate on a pillow
till my personal power gives me a hicky.

I could never marry you.
In my past life I was a rhinoceros
involved in a hideous stampede,
and you were the elephant I trampled.

I could never marry you.
My karma includes a lot of fasting.
It'll take me five more lifetimes
just to let you feed me grapes.

I could never marry you,
but I would accept a phone call.
You could try about 10:30
when my answering machine has a date.

SUBMISSION

It is the dreamy now morning
and sleep has left its stiff mark
on my face. Getting up has to
do with floating from one world

to the next. There are objects
to forget. There are bodies
just out of focus, still calling
from the other side.

They want me to release them,
yet most are trapped under my skin.
I feed them coffee and oranges.
They know things no one is proud of.

I step into my clothes
as a kind of prayer of balance,
a container to keep the edge on things.
They bubble inside my slip.

Violet is the color of healing,
so I dress the night wounds,
pull the wool over my own eyes
or sparkle into my black tights.

MEMO

I think things are falling.
I noticed it this morning
when the wind shook the ash in my yard.
Each leaf made an arc

that curled all the way
from my kitchen window
to the ferns in your garden.
"Cross inspiration," I thought,

and pinned a note to my heart.
These allusions settle me,
so I poured a cup of Kukicha tea
and drank in the trees.

HIGH SKY AND MOVING WATER

You look at me across a menu
at the Midtown Cafe
as if I am Lake Michigan
at Macatawa and you

are about to be caught
in the waves, the great
undertow. The fear of drowning
clearly smarts in your eye.

And I order whitefish,
act as if I don't notice.
Your radical aliveness
clashes with my own trembling.

I want to say something perfect,
wow you into knowing who I am.
Instead I act like Clarabell
and honk my horn three times.

Words don't seem to fit here,
so I talk about my damaged cornea,
how I wear dime store reading glasses,
try to see things a new way.

I feel you leaning toward me,
and I mentally pack my suitcase,
get out of town real fast
before one of us starts falling.

I say ,"Perhaps time is a circle,"
which makes you look at your watch.
You suddenly get nervous.
"People will be wondering
where I am," you say.

I, too, am in a hurry.
We both rush to our cars.
My white Mazda feels like a sailboat
floating down Woodward Avenue,
the wind arching me home.

A MAN COMES TO THE HOUSE

He isn't wearing any shoes.
He just opens the door and walks in when I am
not looking, when I am
busy making biscuits for my bird.

The man comes closer and touches my arm.
It feels like star sounds, and the darkness
around my arm grows quiet. "Watch me,"
he says. "I'm only listening and I won't make

much noise." Something rattles in my
chest. There are openings smaller than the door
to my bird's wooden cage. The man asks me
why my wings make so much noise.

"I think some wild bird has built
a nest in my chimney," I sing.
I am watching the man's whiskers
as I sing that, and he thanks me
for my attention.

I wait to see what he will notice
about my arm. I can't find my arm
anymore, so I wait for him to notice that.
Meanwhile, the bird in my chimney
lays eggs, and they are hatching each day

and the flutter of tiny bird songs
comes drifting through my kitchen
as I am stirring my split pea soup.
The man says he wants to eat the soup

and he waits for me to notice
his hunger, and how very much the soup
is what he wants. And he waits
for me to find my arm, so I can feed him.

As my arm emerges, I notice the flutter
of tiny bird wings now inside the arm.
I start ladling soup all over the floor.
Then I take off my shoes, and we both

walk all around in the soup and begin
to dance. We are dancing just that way
when the star noises come back, and we both
notice them this time. And we both sing.

SCENE

The eyes of the gnarled
tree open into the earth. What does
the tree see in there? How deep can
it peer to the inside story? Leaves,
crumbled and torn, are like tears that
glisten in each bark eye.

Your eyes are like that sometimes.
I feel you watching me so deeply you get
lost and can't find your way out.

I have my own tree eyes.
They go into the center of things,
through the maze of dreams
like those bushes in England.
"I call to them, "Eyes, you're
up to your old tricks again.
How do you ever get out, you old lookers,
who know more than you know about things?"

A tree might lean any way at all, or sparkle
like your brown eyes, opening out as the light does,
in all directions at once.

NEW YORK SKY LINES

The elevator man
knew all about us.
"Going up?" he'd say
and wink at my shy suitcase.

Everything felt Spanish
that week, going up and down
to your place, where the clouds
were painted right on the walls.

"Eleven, please," I'd say
and soak in the colors of the sky.
The motion of my body rising
felt like silver night wings.

There were dreams I couldn't mention
forming right behind my eyes.
He allowed me this private joy.
He didn't say another word.

BUILDING BRIDGES

You left your teeth in my powder room.
I didn't notice at first, but then
the whispering grew louder. I had
to put them in a glass of water

so I could get a little sleep.
Even under water, they began to croon,
"Is it true what they say about dentures?
Do the teeth really shine all the time?"

What to do with these insistent questions
became my newest obsession.
On Monday morning, while I was brushing,
the teeth in the glass made an overture.

They said they'd been secretly watching me floss
and were really getting turned on.
Buoyed by this voyeurist's flattery,
I began to spend hours on my dental hygiene.

Brushing became a precoital dance
with secrets only our teeth could understand.
I even took to eating pop corn and apples
so there'd be more layers to remove.

We've gone too far to turn back now.
We're riding in gondolas down the root canal
and violins are playing "Ebb Tide".
I'm about to blow my VisaCard balance

on a new water pic. Oh, God,
the oral fantasies are endless.
This morning you called to say
you want your bridge work back.

Don't bother me. I'm having
a meaningful relationship with your teeth.
We chatter on about all our past involvements.
I've even confessed my two years of orthodontic

work that failed. This must be truth, or love,
or have we finally bitten off
more than our missing parts can chew?

GIGGLING IN BED

Under the goose down quilt
we roll and squirm,
wiggling like wild kids put to bed.
We snort and chortle
till the whole bed shakes.

Then the room begins to rumble
and wheeze. I bury
my face in your chest;
explosions of air fly
up through my nose.

Skin everywhere, we gasp
for each other.

FEELING OUR WAY

How do I get over this ragging moon?
Can't I see that it is too late
for your call, or just too early?
You are somewhere walking lit streets,
peering in windows of past living rooms,
waiting to see what you will do next.

Neither one of us knows where to start
this suggested waltz between us.
We go to our corners and come out sighing.
Something fundamental lingers on our tongues,
as we eat Chinese or Ethiopian.
Old movies are playing in reverse, or fast forward.

We nearly give each other gifts,
but hold out for the given moment.
The merging question looms large
in the sunset over the city towers.
How do we know this is not dying?
How do we dare open to this life?

MY WELCOME HOME ILLUSION

(for Adam)

It is your magic show,
my son, holding this day
in your hand like a rubber ball.
Yesterday is another red ball

on the table,
covered with a plastic cup.
Abracadabra, you say,
moving time around,

watch my hands, Mother.
And I wonder how you know this.
Today is your welcome home illusion,
you say. My eyes open to it.

I watch the balls vanish
into air, the plastic cups
empty themselves.
It's a winter afternoon.

You wave your silk scarves
at me, and the balls
multiply, then cups, then
tables and years.

I see you
in the middle of your act.
Now you trick me.
Now you don't.

ALLOWING IT TO HAPPEN

(for Mark)

I watch my son
walk out of the lake
with a man's legs on.

I see his body
rumble into shape
while the rest of him
fights back.

I look for the first time
at a stranger on my couch
knowing I still don't
see him.

I watch him walk
through closed doors
with his new power.

I hear the small
creaking of the walls
in his room at night
as he grows
through them.

INDIAN SUMMER

I love my son Erik's hands.
They put together broken things.
Last summer, he came home
and cleaned up the whole downstairs.

I said I'd pay him $4.00 an hour,
but our figures got all tangled.
He forgot to write down the hours,
and I had to make up what I owed.

Nothing seemed like enough,
as he rearranged all our furniture.
I could hear him whistling old Beatles tunes.
Once he sang out, "You can't always get what
you want," while he organized the spices.

When he was born, the first thing I saw
were his hands. "The long, thin fingers
of a piano man," I said to the doctor.
That was the beginning of how

it is with him. He has an eye
for putting together the big picture.
On a sketch pad, or just in his
mind's eye, he gets all the lines connected.

I thought our whole house broke up
when his father and I did.
Now, slowly, by chair and table,
little book shelf, and goose-necked lamp,

he's started us all moving.
Out of the chaos, the burned out
hole in our hearts, is growing
the new order. The breakfast table

now faces east. In October
we eat pasta, and take pleasure
in the new sauce.

NON SEQUITUR

(for Edwin 0. Grahn   1915-1985)

I hold down the trees
while rain tickles the sumac leaves,
scatters them over the grass.

This is the first turning
of green to brown and red
since my father finished his dying.

How the earth turned
one more time around without him
helps me know about seasons.

"If heaven's just a hoax,"
he told me, "I'm coming right back.
But if this is how dying feels,
it's not so bad." He winked

"I feel like a millionaire"
at a nurse who came in
gravely to change his bed pan.
"Our family's awfully good at this.
We ought to do it again sometime."

I watched him twinkle with tubes in his nose,
saying good-bye to his brother Bert.
He grinned at his lime jello and chicken broth lunch,
mumbled something about missing the radishes.

Tourists drove to Traverse City
to witness the colors at their peak.
We watched the blaze out his hospital window,
and Mother said, trying to freeze-frame it,

"Maybe if no wind blows
the leaves will stay on the trees."
We stood around his bed
and made promises to meet him

on the other side for a family picnic.
He told me to bring the potato salad.
We watched him close his eyes and fade.
Susan asked him to pass the olives.

LOVE LETTERS

I LETTER TO FIRE

Dear Red.
I resist you and I can't get
soft. Going into fires
has always named me.

I dance inside the blue
center of the dragon tongue,
since going for the root
gets all the neighbors nervous.

You are my log lover.
I go for the burn,
enter you for exercise,
high impact aerobics of the heart.

II LETTER TO WATER

Dear Breast Stroker.
Face down, you seduce me.
I can't do the dead
woman's float.

Nothing pulls the sheets
like your electric Niagra.
You river me,
and I sift upstream.

I want to sail into your
rapids, rolling over the dam
life jacket that fits
my belly deep slough.

III LETTER TO AIR

Dear Gasp.
Get inside my pants.
Breeze me up with
breath that kisses feet.

Be my buoy friend
and take me flying.
Let's do some dangerous
loops in altitude.

Let's get tornado
tongued on hurricanes.
I'm a wind stalker;
come lift my skirt.

IV LETTER TO EARTH

Dear Dirt.
I really dig your eyes.
You mulch my inner
sod story. I get

fertile fantasies at night.
Be my hanging planter.
I'm a child making mud
pie memories come true.

I'll go down for your
roots in my garden.
As the worm turns,
bloom me up.

ABOUT THE AUTHOR:

Margo LaGattuta lives in Rochester, Michigan, with her three sons. Her first two collections of poetry are DIVERSION ROAD, a chapbook from State Street Press, New York, 1983; and NOEDGELINES, a collaborations with visual artist Chris Reising from Earhart Press, Ann Arbor, Michigan, 1986.

She has an MFA in poetry from Vermont College, and teaches writing and creative process workshops at Oakland Community College, Cranbrook, Keller Clinic, Macomb Community College, and the Lawrence Street Gallery. She is the founder and director of the HEARD program, an alternative teaching program in Pontiac, Michigan.

She has often used a dream circle in her writing workshops, where the group discusses dreams, shares associations, then uses them to stimulate writing.

Margo has produced an audio tape called THE CREATIVE PROCESS - DEVELOPING THE RIGHT BRAIN, which is available both from LAKE SHORE PUBLISHING and Inventing The Invisible, 29 W. Lawrence, Pontiac, MI 48342.

ACKNOWLEDGEMENTS

Jesus At The Outlet and Looking For Elvis In Kalamazoo, H.M. at Midwest Poetry Festival, Lansing, MI; Deaf Kitten, The Blind Woman's House, published in PASSAGES NORTH; To Natalie Wood As She Is Leaving The Boat, for Quadra Project, 1984 Calendar; Painting Faces, in CALLIOPE; Scene, and Feeling Our Way, in MOBIUS; Nothing Lies Like The Truth, and The Fallen Mouth Over Long Windows, in RENEGADE; My Welcome Home Illusion, in DIVERSION ROAD; The Wish Bracelet, in TEE BRIDGE; Memo, 1st place, Ohio Poetry Day; Riding Tough Horses, in METRO TIMES; Allowing It To Happen, in GREEN RIVER REVIEW.

I wish to thank the Ragdale Foundation, Lake Forest, Illinois, where this book was completed.